TOKYO
SPORTS CENTER OF THE ORIENT

東洋のスポーツの中心地
東　京
―1940年幻の東京オリンピック招致アルバム―

Edited & Introduced by
Hisashi Sanada

監修
真田　久（筑波大学教授）

Tokyo:
Kyokuto Shoten Ltd.

2018

This edition published by Kyokuto Shoten, 2018

Kyokuto Shoten, Ltd.

2-7-10 Misakicho

Chiyoda-ku, Tokyo 101-8672, Japan

ISBN 978-4-87394-025-0

The quality of this reprint is equivalent to

the quality of the original work

Printed and bound in Japan by

Fuji Repro Ltd.

目次

解説

招請状

東洋のスポーツの中心地　東京……………………(i)

東京の競技施設

東京と第12回オリンピアード

オリンピック競技大会に理想的な気候

大東京…………………………………………(iv)

東京の成り立ち

東京の復興

都市範囲及び人口の急速な拡大

現在も続く改良

寺社仏閣、公園

近代的な建物

公衆衛生

教育機関

社会事業

近代的な給水設備

交通施設

ホテル宿泊設備

日本の第二言語、英語

娯楽施設

東京に来ませんか？

Contents

INVITATION

TOKYO: SPORTS CENTER OF THE ORIENT……………i

Tokyo's Facilities for Sports

Tokyo and the 12th Olympiad

The Ideal Weather for Olympic Games

GREATER TOKYO……………………………………iii

Tokyo's Origin

Tokyo's Reconstruction

Rapid Expansion in Area and Population

Modern Improvements

Temples, Shrines and Parks

Modern Buildings

Public Health

Educational Facilities

Social Works

Modern Water Supply System

Traffic Facilities

Hotel Accommodation

English, The Second Language in Japan

Recreation Facilities

Will You Be There?

解　説

真田　久（筑波大学教授）

　本書は、1933（昭和8）年に東京市により発行され、当時の国際オリンピック委員会（IOC）委員に配布された写真集である。その内容は、永田秀次郎東京市長による、オリンピック開催地立候補の表明が記され、その後に、東京で開催することの意義と課題が8ページにわたり説明されている。

　この書に掲載された写真は、皇居や国会議事堂、丸の内オフィス街や日比谷公園、隅田公園、銀座や新宿などの繁華街などである。東京市内の競技施設としては、明治神宮外苑競技場やプール、さらに冬季オリンピックの会場として札幌の大倉山シャンツェなども掲載され、それらの施設で様々なスポーツに興じている市民の様子が紹介されている。柔道、剣道、弓道などの伝統的スポーツも紹介されている。これらの写真は大日本体育協会、鉄道省、講道館、東京朝日新聞、東京日日新聞が提供したものである。この写真集は、日本人IOC委員嘉納治五郎により、1934年5月にアテネで開催されたIOC総会で配布された。
日本がIOC委員にオリンピック招致を目指して配布した最初の写真集である。

　東京市長永田秀次郎が招致をIOCに向けて表明したのは1932年7月であり、翌1933年の3月、日本は満州国問題により国際連盟脱退を表明、世界の孤児になりつつあった時であった。このような折に、東京でのオリンピック開催をIOCに訴え始めたのであった。永田市長は東洋での初開催を希望するとともに、オリンピックムーブメントへ貢献することを掲げている。スポーツの分野では、世界とのつながりを深めようとしていたのである。

　本書での東京での開催のビジョンを説明するくだりでは、オリンピックの時代的経過とともに、優勝者や入賞者の国籍が広がり、着実にスポーツの国際的発展がなされつつあること、その中で東洋での開催がそうした傾向をさらに強めるであろうことを示唆している。

　東京開催の課題として、本書では、競技施設、宿泊施設、人々の関心、そして天候があげられている。東京は1933年5月には人口540万人を越え、ニューヨーク、ロンドンにつぐ世界三番目の大都市になっていた。競技施設は明治神宮外苑競技場を中心に、陸上競技場やプール、球技場など多様な施設が存在していること、宿泊施設も十分に準備できること、そして国民のスポーツへの関心も高く「スポーツ狂」であること、などが言及されている。また天候は、梅雨明けの7月下旬から8月初旬の期間が安定していて最適であると述べられている。

東京の魅力として、西洋的な近代都市が備えている交通体系、公共建築物、ホテル、交通網、水道水、学校、図書館、映画館などが完備しているとともに、日本の伝統的な文化である寺社、庭園、滝、木々なども調和的に存在しており、そのことが西洋人に驚きの感慨をもたらすだろうと述べている。（2020年の東京オリンピック・パラリンピック競技大会の立候補ファイルについて、IOC評価委員会が評価したことの一つは、この点であった。）

　また、1923年9月に起きた関東大震災により、東京市は火災によって半分が焼失したが、その後の復興努力により、東京は以前にも増して美しく耐久性の強い都市になったと言及されている。その証として、耐震構造の学校が117校建てられ、大小の公園も100余りに増えた。中でも明治神宮外苑はスポーツの中心的競技場として発展している様子が示され、大震災後におけるスポーツによる復興が暗示されている。関東大震災が起きた時の東京市長も永田秀次郎であり、後藤新平復興院総裁とともに、嘉納治五郎の提案を受け入れて、隅田、浜町、錦糸公園造営の折にプール、テニスコート、児童公園などのスポーツ施設を設けたのであった。復興した東京でオリンピックを開催することは、スポーツによる復興の成果を示すことでもあったのである。

　スポーツによる復興は、第二次世界大戦による復興を印象付けた1964年の東京オリンピック、そして2020年の東京オリンピック、パラリンピックのビジョンにも通じるものである。3回の東京招致を通して、復興という共通のビジョンに言及されていることは、まことに興味深い。

　日本人が初めてオリンピックを招致しようとした時、どのように東京をアピールし、どのようなビジョンを世界に訴え、そしてオリンピックムーブメントに貢献しようとしたのか。そのことを知るために、本書は貴重なオリンピックの史料となろう。

東洋のスポーツの中心地
東 京

東京市役所

1933年

写真は、大日本体育協会、鉄道省、
講道館、東京朝日新聞、
東京日日新聞
の提供による

印刷：大塚工藝社（東京）

招　請　状

国際オリンピック委員会

拝啓

　東京市および東京市民を代表し、下記署名の東京市長たる私は、国際オリンピック委員会に対して、1940年に第12回オリンピック競技大会が日本で開催され、東京がオリンピック都市として選ばれるよう、謹んで招請申し上げるものであります。東京市職員、市民、日本の企業および競技団体はこぞって招請に賛同の意を示しております。

　私どもは、第12回オリンピアードを開催する栄誉と喜びが与えられることを切望し、成功の暁には近代オリンピックの歴史において注目に値する大会とする所存であります。また、1940年は皇紀2600年にあたる年でもあり、その機をとらえてオリンピック・ムーブメントに比類のない貢献を果たす決意であります。

　東京市は、オリンピック競技大会の成功に向けて責任を果たすために真摯に取り組むことをここに確約します。1940年のオリンピック都市に東京が選ばれた時には、第12回オリンピアードにおいて卓越した輝かしい成果が得られるよう、あらゆる面で最善を尽くします。

　聖火が東洋への道を照らさんことを。そして我々の親密な関係が、人類のために国と国との相互理解をさらに深め、より純粋で、熱く、さらなる勇気に満ちた友情が育まれんことを祈りつつ。

敬具

東京市長
永田　秀次郎

東京、1932年7月9日

東洋のスポーツの中心地
東京

人類の発展の歴史において破滅的な出来事とも呼ぶべき世界大戦が終わって、スポーツに対する関心は世界中で高まってきた。人間は本質的に競争を好み、その自然な欲求を理解する近代国家の指導者には、スポーツを奨励し、心身の健全さ、健康、健やかさという目標に沿って実施されるようにする賢明さがあった。その結果が近代的な意味におけるスポーツの発展である。それは、可能な限り最高のスピード、最高の律動、最高のパフォーマンスまで身体能力を高める努力と定義することができる。それは運動本来の性質である楽しさを享受するために脳と筋肉を鍛えるだけでなく、完全性、すなわち最高の結果を追求するということだ。

この国際的な発展は、一ヶ国、または一大陸に限られたものではない。今や世界中に広がっている。1896年にアテネでオリンピック競技大会が復活したときは、そうではなかった。予定された14種目の内、9種目で米国、3種目で英国が勝利した。英国と米国はその当時まで、スポーツと言えばいずれかの名前が挙がる存在であり、他の国はまだあまりスポーツに力を注いでいなかった。両国によるこの支配は世界大戦まで続いたが、アントワープ、パリ、アムステルダム、ロサンゼルスにおいて、スポーツに関心を持つ地域の広がりが徐々に明らかになっていった。これら4つのオリンピアードでは、すべての大陸から優勝者が出た。ロサンゼルスでは、様々な種目の団体競技で7つの異なる国が優勝し、1位、2位、または3位で表彰されたチームは15ヶ国に上った。また、39ヶ国の内29ヶ国が入賞を果たした。そして、勝利の冠を戴いた優勝者の国籍は18ヶ国に及んだ。

ロサンゼルスで各国が示した成果は、世界全体がスポーツに真剣に取り組んでいることの現れだった。趣味本位（ディレッタンティズム）は消え去り、トレーニングには徹底した研究が生かされるようになった。国家は、トレーニング、気候、その他の条件、および競技施設に重点を置き、オリンピアード開催国になることを想定したとき、その条件を満たせる能力に自信を持てなければならない。しかし、東洋のスポーツの中心地である東京にはその自信があり、近代における第12回オリンピアードが開催される1940年に、世界各国を客人として招きたいと考える。この本書の目的は、日本の首都が有する、開催国の栄誉を受ける適切性を示すことである。

何点か検討すべき問題がある。第一は競技施設の問題となろう。第二は、公衆向けの宿泊施設に関してである。第三は世間からの関心の問題、第四が天候の問題である。

東京の競技施設

東京の競技施設は最高の国際基準を満たしており、今日にでも世界中の選手を迎える用意がある。この日本第一の都市は、人口540万人を擁する首都であり、世界第三の大都市である。そのスポーツの中心地は明治神宮外苑である。これは、1912年に崩御された明治天皇を祀る明治神宮を取り巻く公園である。明治天皇は大日本帝国を西洋文明に開き、1912年までこの国を導いた。この外苑には、世界のいかなる施設にも引けを取らない運動施設がある。二つの大競技場の内、一つは陸上競技、ラグビー、サッカー、その他類似する競技用（収容人数：6万人）であり、もう一つは野球用（収容人数：5万5千人）で、年間を通して観客で賑わう。これに隣接して、明治神宮プール（収容人数：1万5千人）がある。これは、我が国の水泳選手らがロサンゼルスで体験したものとできる限り近い条件を選手らに与えようという目的で建設された。

東京を縦断する隅田川では、レガッタの大学対抗レースが開催される。この水上の祭典は首都の毎年の恒例行事であるため、コース沿いには観客のために十分な施設がある。下流に横たわる東京湾へと続く水流は概して穏やかで、ほぼ完全に内陸に位置しており、7月及び8月初旬の状態は、六大陸の漕ぎ手にとって理想的と言えるだろう。

ヨットに使用できるコースは二つある。一つは東京湾下部、もう一つは三浦半島の西である。三浦半島の方ではおそらく、より大きな船が出帆できるだろう。いずれも首都から1時間圏内である。

東京の境界地域にはカントリークラブが点在しており、軍隊の訓練場はさらに多くある。そのため、乗馬及び射撃種目に関しても、現時点で十分に対応が可能である。レスリング、フェンシング、ボクシング、ウェイトリフティング、体操などの室内競技に関しても同様となる。しかしながら、国際オリンピック委員会が1940年の開催国として東京を指名するならば、これらすべての設備は全面的に改良され、集約化のための努力がなされ、世界中のスポーツ選手の到着を歓迎する施設は、想像し得る限り完璧なものになるだろう。現時点でも既に卓越した環境がある。工事の多くは、想定される記録的な群衆に見合う空間を提供するために行われることになろう。

東京と第12回オリンピアード

これまでにオリンピアードが開催されたすべての国における最大の懸念事項は国民による支援だった。ロサンゼルスまで、黒字のオリンピアードはなかった。しかし東京には、その点に関する心配はない。というのも、この国の民は、文字通り「スポーツ狂（sports-mad）」だからである。この国には、経済的に自立していない近代スポーツは存在しない。陸上競技、ラグビー、陸上ホッケー、フットボールの小規模な大学対抗試合は、米国やその他の国々では不人気と悪名が高いが、それさえこの国では何万もの熱心な支持者を引きつけている。東京が1940年のオリンピアード開催国になれば、全種目にわたっ

てほぼすべての座席が高額であっても買われるであろう。1932年6月、2隻の船で出発する日本選手の幸運を祈る群衆や大会のニュースに熱中する人々の様子を目の当たりにし、選手たちが帰国した際の、国中の心からの歓喜を体験したならば、大日本帝国が身分の隔てなく国を挙げて、東京で開催される競技大会を支援することを疑う者はいないはずである。

無論、気候の問題が存在する。この点については、ほぼすべての観点から理想的とみなすことができる。冬季競技には、日本アルプスの固く締まった雪原がある。ここは、冬の多くの月を通じてスキー及びスケートに理想的なフィールドである。この地域へは、東京から直結する快適な鉄道路線でわずか4、5時間で行ける。観客及び選手向けの宿泊施設には改良が必要だが、スキーコースは既にヨーロッパの高い基準に達している。

オリンピック競技大会に理想的な気候

天候の観点から言えば、7月下旬から8月初旬にかけてはおそらく、日本で最も安定している時期である。「7月が来ると梅雨が明ける」ということわざがある。常にそうとは言えないが、少なくとも7月の第一週には梅雨が明ける。それ以降、8月中旬まで、東京は概ね、あらゆる種類の運動競技にとって事実上完全な、安定した晴天に恵まれる。台風シーズンによる強風と不安定な天候は、8月中旬過ぎまで始まらない。

これらはもちろん、東京が自らを1940年のオリンピアードにふさわしい開催国であると信じる主たる理由である。しかし他の、はるかに重要な理由がある。

現在、スポーツへの関心は世界中に広まっており、東洋は既に国際オリンピック委員会から認められるに値する、オリンピックへの忠誠と運動能力を十分に示したという事実がある。これこそが、我々が臆することなくこれほどの強調をする理由である。我々は、すべてのスポーツ機関によって認められていることを信じている。

日本はオリンピック競技大会にとって、類い稀な興味深い環境であり、世界はこの事実に無知ではいられない。西洋文明に開かれてわずか60年、いまだ多くの古いものが残っている。そこには、鮮やかで興味深い対照がある。他の理由はなくとも、この理由で、世界は日本に関心を寄せている。この数千年にわたる文明を背景として、また、単一の皇室による皇紀2600年記念を祝う国家行事が行われるこの機会に第12回オリンピアードを開催することは、競技大会に対するさらなる関心を喚起し、相乗的な魅力を付加するだろう。

日本はもはや、世界の果てではない。輸送手段の発達により、日本へはオーストラリアを除くあらゆる参加国から2週間以内で来られるようになった。そのオーストラリアにしても、欧州や米国からの方が日本から行くよりも遠いのである。太平洋は世界の中央にあり、日本はその太平洋の中心にある。そして東京は、地理的、文化的、経済的に、さらにスポーツという観点においても、日本の中心である。

大　東　京

日本と西洋の慣習の違いがあまりにも強調されてきたため、来日した外国人は東京の近代性に対する驚きはなかなか拭い去れないほどである。日本を訪れた外国人は、なだらかな丘陵地帯に広がる近代的な都市、美しい公共建築物、すばらしい商業施設、管理の行き届いた道路、効率的かつ高速の送電線や路面電車、多数のタクシー、世界のどこにも引けを取らない水道システム、西洋式の快適なホテル、公園、学校、工場、映画館など、まさに西洋文化に付随するものとして慣れ親しんだあらゆるものを目にするだろう。

　日本の大工は家を建てるときにまず屋根を作る、鉋（かんな）やのこぎりを西洋式に押すのではなく自分の方へ引いて使う、書物は左から右ではなく上から下に印刷されている、といった限定的な知識のみを書物から得ているなら、あるいは、芸者、寺、神社、木々に囲まれた滝、日常の喧噪からかけ離れた静謐な庭、儒教、武士道、四十七士、あらゆる語句の前に置かれる敬語などが、多くの空想的な書き手が誤って主張しているようなイメージで混然一体となっているようなら、東京に着いたとき、その先入観が受ける衝撃は、極めて大きいに違いない。

　この点について誤解があってはならない。日本には古代からの文明があり、我々はそれに誇りを持っている。それは、大日本帝国があらゆる手段で守るであろう、文化的遺産である。だが、文化とは、およそ無形のものである。それは来訪者の目の前に突き出されるものではない。今日の日本は近代国家である。日本は、自らの必要性に最もよく適合すると思われる西洋の進歩の特質を選び、取り入れ、一部には改良を加えた。今日の東京は、世界で最も美しい都市の一つである。確かに、古い日本の多くの部分はまだ残っているが、それは外見ではなく、人々の心の奥底に存在している。今も古い時代の空気が流れる寺社がある。そこは、数千年にわたる宗教的な隔絶から生まれた強い信仰心と畏敬の念を伴う学識で満ちている。しかし、日本の心の基盤は過去にあるとしても、その体は現在を歩んでおり、その目は未来を見据えている。そしてそのリーダーは、東京である。

東京の成り立ち　東京は今から千年程前、文化の花が咲く京都や奈良から遠く離れた、日本の東の端の荒れ地だった。その後、小さな村ができ、466年前、封建制度の領主であった太田道灌が、自らの城を築く場所として、戦略的理由からこの地を選んだ。1590年には、当時の東京の呼び名であった江戸の近辺の関八州が大大名の徳川家康に与えられた。その10年後、家康は日本全体の将軍（軍の長）となり、江戸を首都に選んだ。家康は各国の大名たちを家族の下

を離れて江戸に来させ、一時期を江戸で過ごすように命じた。これと同時に、両替商や商人を誘致し、江戸に本拠地を置かせた。このようにして江戸には人々が押し寄せ、取るに足らない寒村の状態から時の首都へと発展していった。無論、本当の首都は朝廷がある京都のままであったが、商売や政治の中心は東に集約された。徳川の将軍によるこの体制は、明治維新が起きる1868年まで、268年間続いた。この体制が終了したとき、明治天皇は東京と名を変えた江戸に首都を移し、将軍の城を皇居とした。東京とは、「東の都」という意味である。

東京の現在の繁栄への道筋を説明することは近代日本について語ることであり、本書では到底語りきれない。しかし、日本の西洋世界への扉は明治維新によって開かれ、またこのとき、新たな日本の支配者は未知の文明の中に価値を見出し導入を決断したことを明記しておかなければならない。発展は怒涛のように始まった。1870年、初の電灯工場が設置され、操業を開始した。1872年には、日本初の鉄道が東京から横浜港までの14マイルの区間で開通した。こうした小さな始まりから、日本とその首都の発展は、1923年までは着実かつ急速に進んだ。だが、この年の9月1日の午前11時58分、地震が発生し、130カ所以上で火災が起こり、東京の半分以上が破壊された。約30万棟の家屋やビルが倒壊又は焼失し、被害額は推定37億円（3億7千万ポンド、18億5千万ドル、74億ドイツマルクに相当）とされる。

東京の復興

大火災の後は常に、災厄の中にも神の恵みはあるということがよく言われる。東京に関して言えば、これは文字通り真実だった。大火災当時、行政担当者たちは、街の美化、道幅の拡充、建築物や公共物その他の特性の改良を狙いとした都市基本計画を策定していた。そのようなとき、地震は価値ある教訓をもたらした。それは、鉄筋コンクリートによる近代建築は実際に衝撃に強いことを示した。このようにして、火災の残り火がまだくすぶる中、復興後の東京をより美しく、安全な場所にするための指示が出された。市民は、特定の区域においては暫定的な建物のみ、建設を許可された。その後、新たな道路が作られ、恒久的な建物の建設が許可された。一部区域では、鉄骨及び鉄筋コンクリートの建築物のみが許可された。東京は、7億円以上を費やし、一部は直接、一部は助成金や、道路の拡充や町の改良のために私有地を接収された所有者への補償金という形で支払われた。その結果が、広い道路が走り、コンクリートの建物で四角く区切られた沢山の小さな区域から成る1933年の東京である。この先、この大都市が1923年のように端から端まで火災に燃えつくされるようなことはないだろう。

この件について注視重要である。1923年の地震は、最悪のタイミングで発生した。というのも、東京中の主婦がこのとき昼食の支度中で、何万ものコンロに火が点いていたのである。地震の振動でコンロはひっくり返り、多数の火災が発生した。地震の発生がもう30分早かったら、あるいは30分遅

(v)

かったら、実質的な損害はこれほど甚大ではなかっただろう。実際、東京では地震により倒壊した家屋は焼失したよりもはるかに少なかった。このように、同じような災害が繰り返される可能性は小さく、現在でも行政者たちの賢明な都市計画により、その可能性をより小さくする努力が続けられている。

都市範囲及び人口の急速な拡大

1920年の人口調査と1930年の人口調査の間に、東京の人口は10万人しか増えていない。これは一部には1923年の地震と火災が原因だが、主たる要因は、交通機関の発達により、郊外からの通勤が可能になっただけでなく、望まれるようになったことにある。この間の10年で、郊外には173万人の住民が増え、東京そのものよりも多い人口増加となった。郊外には、84の町や村が存在した。年月の経過とともに、これらのコミュニティが東京との合併により受ける恩恵は益々明白になり、首都の自治が34年に達した1932年の10月1日、これらの内82の町村が東京に編入された。新たに20区が置かれ、併せて35区となり、東京市の範囲は85平方キロメートルから553平方キロメートルへと拡大した。東京市の半径は、東京駅を中心として10マイルである。最新の国勢調査の実施日である1930年10月1日時点で、東京に含まれる区域の人口は4,970,839人に上る。1932年10月1日までに、この数は5,298,957人まで増加し、1933年の5月現在、確実に5,400,000人を超えた。そして今や東京は大ロンドンとニューヨークに次ぐ世界第三の都市になり、ベルリンとシカゴを抜いた。

現在も続く改良

東京における建設及び改良は完了していない。現在の東京市はすばらしい状態にあり、過去に経験した試練の影は見られないが、当局はこれに満足せず、今後15年間にわたり、8億6千万円以上を費やす計画を立てている。この総額の内3億3千万円は、道路と橋の建設に充てられる。東京は現在、包括的な道路建設計画を実施中である。この計画が完了した暁には、東京は世界で最もよく整備された都市の一つになるだろう。地震の前、東京市の道路の総面積は、925,621平方マイルだった。新計画が完了したら、この面積はほぼ4倍の3,600,000平方マイルまで増えるだろう。道幅33～44メートルの基幹道路が南北に走る予定である。これは現在、ほぼ完成しており、ほとんどの部分が既に使用されている。さらに、ほぼ同じ道幅の横方向の幹線道路も通る。これら両方の幹線道路の側面には、混雑緩和のために、やや狭い道路が配置される。東京市を取り囲む大規模な幹線道路は今後4～5年の間に完成し、東京駅に向かう放射状の大通りとつながる計画である。この計画は都市計画の心臓部となっている。これらに加え、東京市中に道幅22メートル以上、全長119キロメートルに及ぶ52の通りが建設され、より小さな、又は道幅22メートル未満の122の通りによって補完される。道路計画の完了時には、対象区域の27％を道路が占めるだろう。これは、ロンドン、パリ、ベルリンに勝るとも劣らない数字である。この工事のほとんどは、1940年のオリンピアードで東京が開催国となるときには完了して

いるだろう。

　東京は橋の多い都市であり、隅田川にはひときわ目立つ9つの大きな橋が架かっている。また、運河が碁盤状に町を区切っており、復興工事中には、523の道路の橋の建設が必要とされた。これらの大部分は、実用面だけでなく、都市美という観点から設計されている。

寺社仏閣、公園　近代都市となる前の東京の生活環境は、特に密集した状態にはなかった。当時の寺や神社には公園が併設され、ほとんどの民家にも庭があった。しかし、不動産価格急騰のあおりを受けて、このような状況を維持することは難しくなり、市当局は都市計画に公園を盛り込むことを余儀なくされた。東京市には現在、公園が100ヶ所あり、その一部はきわめて広大である。中でも明治神宮外苑は、最大の面積を誇り、既述したように2つのスタジアム、水泳プールの他、バスケットボール、ボクシング、フェンシング、レスリング用の野外競技場、その他の施設が設置されている。この地は、広大な代々木練兵場や明治神宮の公園にも隣接している。現在は主に東京の所有地であるが、元々は重要な仏寺の敷地であった芝公園、美術館や博物館、動物園のある上野公園、浅草公園、野外音楽堂や円形劇場を擁する日比谷公園、さらには隅田川下流の両岸の見事な公園などが、東京のどちらかと言えば密集地帯にあって大きく開けた場所である。

近代的な建物　本資料の読者の方々に東京及び市の近代的な施設等の全体像を理解いただくのは難しい。なぜなら、東京市の都市活動やこれまでに達成した進歩・改良は、市民の生活の多様な局面に影響を与えてきたためである。たとえば、3階建ての耐震構造の小学校が117棟あるが、いずれも見事な構造物である。東京帝国大学、慶應大学、早稲田大学、東京文理科大学などの高等教育機関があり、いずれも学術および運動競技をおこなうための卓越した設備が整えられている。庁舎、とりわけ1923年関東大震災以後に建設された建物は、建築家の技能の力量を示す証しとなっている。神宮外苑の美術館や帝国議会議事堂は、日本が誇る近代様式の建物であり、海外の人々の目にも印象的に映るであろう。政府機関を始めとする市の重要な銀行は、日本仕様の西洋建築の成功例である。中でも秀逸な建築物として挙げられるのは、日本銀行、三井銀行、横浜正金銀行、三菱銀行、第一銀行、日本勧業銀行である。これらの建造物に加えて、新しい東京中央郵便局、簡易保険局ビル、丸の内ビル、東京海上保険ビル、東京証券取引所などがあるが、これらの建物の印象は、実際に目にすることで確認ができるものである。これ以上の果てしない建築物の例を挙げることは、いかに美辞麗句を並べても無益なことである。したがって、首都の物理的な側面については本書に添付する写真をご参照願いたい。

公衆衛生　東京には、優秀な設備の整った病院が多数ある。大規模病院としては、1923年の火災・地震後にア

メリカからの寄付で建設された同愛記念病院、皇室からの多大な寄付を受けている日本赤十字社病院、先ごろ新築建物に業務を移した聖路加国際病院がある。これらに加えて、小規模な病院が数十ある。これらの多くは私立病院で豊かな資金源を有している。また、無料の公立病院も数ヶ所あり、合計で1000床、1日の外来患者数は1000人である。

東京の健康・衛生管理は徹底しており、欧州の首都のシステムにも引けを取らない。近年の例でいうと、当局の迅速な対応が奏功し、流行性疾患件数はわずか21,710件のみの報告となっている。これらのうちの半数以上が赤痢で、隣国中国における正に管理不能の状態を考慮すると、健康当局のこの記録は注目すべき成果である。

下水道の敷設工事は、1923年の地震によりかなり遅れを示したが、現在は順調に進んでおり、今後15年で1億9,000万円を投じて整備が進む。廃棄物処理施設は改善してきている。市内各所に27の中継所を設けたことで、ごみ撤去についてはこの10年で大幅な改善が見られた。

教育機関

東京には現在、1,602の教育機関があり、その内訳は公立が842校、私立が760校となっている。これには117の総合大学、単科大学、高等工業学校が含まれる。東京市が運営する幼稚園、小学校、中学校、高等女学校、実業学校が793校あるが、この数には当然のことながら日中は仕事をする貧困家庭の子女のための夜間学校も含まれる。

社会事業

解雇手当に関する日本の法律や習慣はうまく運用されており、ほぼ安定的な雇用が維持されている。したがって、合衆国や欧州を悩ませているような問題はわが国にはないが、公的支援を必要とするような人々はおそらく、どんな時代であってもいるものである。東京における貧民人口は317,090である。過密した生活環境は当然のことながら、公衆衛生の観点からすると常に脅威となることから、市庁はその是正のために最善を尽くしている。現在98の地区福祉事務所、1800の福祉ホームがあり、困窮者が仕事を見つけるための支援と物理的な環境の改善に向けた努力を行っている。東京には921の社会福祉グループがあり、そのうち304が市の管理下にある。

近代的な給水設備

日本では水を煮沸せずに飲んではいけない―どれほど多くの日本を訪れる人たちが無知な旅行者からこのようなことを聞かされていたのだろう？これほど事実からかけ離れたことはない。東京は1911年から、世界のどの国にも引けを取らない給水設備を有している。同年、20年がかりの工事を経て多摩貯水池が完成した。かつては河川の上流から淀橋のろ過池へと導かれていたので、東京は良質の水が保証されていた。しかし、その給水量は当時の人口だから適正であったに過ぎない。当局はこのことを認識し、5年後に都心から40マイルの地にある村山貯水池の工事に着手した。1926年にこのプロジェクトが完成したので旧東京（1932年の合併前）には適正な給水量である。だが、現在

2つの別な給水工事が進行中で、東京市に含まれる町村全域にも年間を通して十分な量の清水が供給される予定である。

交通施設　東京の道路、公園、建物の観点からの最新の状況については十分述べてきた。さて、交通施設はどうだろうか。施設は完成し包括的である。鉄道省の電車が市内を環状に走り、近隣市のすべてに短時間かつ便利に接続している。中心部を走る環状線の全長は96キロメートルである。東京には、民間会社による200キロメートルに及ぶ私鉄が走るほか、路面電車やバス路線もある。これらの交通施設の1年あたりの乗客数は10億人を超える。一大娯楽センターである浅草公園から市の中心部までの地下鉄もある。この地下鉄の運営会社の報告によると、最初に2マイル部分が開通した時から安定的に利益を計上しており、第12回オリンピアードが東京で開催されるまでには、同社の計画は順調に進行するはずだとしている。この計画とは、市の中心部を環状に結び、支線が中心部から首都圏の各所に数分で接続するというものである。当該計画は1940年には大いに有効なものとなるはずである。たとえば、これから建設されるオリンピック・スタジアムまでホテルやビジネス中心街からタクシーで20分、鉄道省の電車では30分かかるところを地下鉄であれば6～7分で結ぶというのだから。

　輸送路には、当然のことながら航空輸送も含まれる。東京またはその近辺に3つの飛行場があるが、どのホテルにも最も便利なのは羽田空港である。

ホテル宿泊設備　東京の支援者がどれほど楽観主義者だったとしても、1940年に東京が選ばれた場合に、現状からするとオリンピックに押し寄せる人たちの宿泊を受け入れられるほどのホテルのスペースがないことを認めざるを得ないだろう。だが、世界の他の都市同様、東京市とその周辺地域にも、解決の手立てがある。東京には西洋式のホテルは6つしかないが、幸いなことにすぐ近くの日本の玄関口にリゾート地として人気の高い神奈川県が控えている。同県には、海外からの客のもてなしにかけては随一といわれる葉山、逗子、鎌倉、宮ノ下、大磯、小田原、箱根などがある。また横浜もその一つだ。このように、大会に訪れる人々は、周辺地区のいたるところにある魅力あふれるホテルでの宿泊が可能である。その多くは、海水浴もできるような地でありながら、都心や国際競技会場から1時間以内なのである。

　当然のことながら、選手のためには特別な宿泊施設が用意され、それらの施設は間違いなく代表団のコーチ、トレーナー、その他役員にも提供されるだろう。オリンピアードを体験しようと海外から訪れる観戦者のための宿泊設備については、東京が開催都市に選ばれたら早々に全力でその準備に着手する予定であり、西欧諸国にあってはご安心願いたい。その枠組みはすでに出来上がっている。

日本の第二言語、英語　読者にとって1つ気になる点があるとしたら、言語のことだろう。これまでオリンピアードは、少なくとも第二言語は競技者や

訪問者の大半になじみのある国々で開催されてきた。選手や訪問者が日本のような国でうまくやっていけるだろうかと否定的なオリンピック役員の姿を思い浮かべるかもしれない。だが、その点は心配無用だ。英語は日本における第二言語である。誰もが流暢に英語を話すとまでは言わないが、選手たちが接することになる大学生はいずれも簡単な会話であれば可能である。ホテルや旅館では、英語を使いこなす者が少なくとも１名は配されている。

娯楽施設

東京には当然のことながら、訪れる人のための娯楽施設が整っている。いわゆる観光名所、寺社仏閣、記念碑、美術館、博物館などだが、これらは日中の名所旧跡である。夜にもまたさまざまな楽しみがある。東京には約12ヶ所の洋画専門のロードショー映画館があり、加えておよそ60ヶ所の小規模な邦画劇場がある。さらに、古い時代の音楽の演奏もある歌舞伎や現代歌舞伎を専門とする劇場もある。西洋式のショーを上演する劇場が２〜３ヶ所あり、こうした劇場の演目は外国人にも理解しやすい。また市の各所に10以上のレビュー小劇場があるが、ここでは大掛かりなものではなく、ユーモアあふれるパントマイムが主たる演目となっている。日本語のわからない外国観光客は往々にして、大劇場でのパリ風の複雑なショーより、こうした娯楽の方がわかりやすく楽しめるようだ。

東京には、10〜12ヶ所のダンスホールがあり、そこではまず間違いなく西洋音楽が流れている。こうしたダンスホールはいずれも警察の厳しい管理下にある。数千からあるバーやカフェの内おそらく100軒くらいは外国人の目に魅力的に映るだろう。市としては、こうした店の存在を誇らしく考えているわけではなく、十分な管理下に置くよう配慮している。だが、キャバレーのような娯楽施設のない我が国を訪れる人々にとって、バーやカフェがきわめて楽しく娯楽的要素にあふれていると思うことを付け加えておくべきだろう。

東京に来ませんか？

ここまでは、近代都市東京の起源、問題点、現状などについて述べてきた。東京は非常に大きな発展を遂げてきており、そして現在も驚異的な速さで前進している。おそらく―そして絶対にありえないことではなく―第12回オリンピアードのトランペットが鳴り響くまでの短い７年間で、日本の首都についてここに述べられてきた貧弱な状況が判別できないほどの変化を遂げるであろう。1940年の東京は、今日の東京が1926年と比べるとほとんど別物のように、大きく変わっていることだろう。

本書では東京がオリンピアードを開催する都市として十分な資格要件を満たしていることを示すことに注力した。東京には完備した運動施設があり、世界でもこれをしのぐ施設はほとんどないといえる。またすぐれた競技記録を有していることもまた開催の栄誉に浴する資格となる。一般民衆は、事業成功を期して海外からの客人に敬意を表し、試合場に集まることであろう。東京は近代的な都市、清潔な都市、古くからの文明を背景とする西洋型のメトロポリスである。近代都

市と古くからの文明という魅力的なコントラストを有する東京は、まさに合理的な計画と勇気ある遂行を日々目の当たりにできる具体的な実例である。東京は近代オリンピック競技大会で最も素晴らしい大会の一つとなるオリンピアード開催を実行する施設を擁する都市であり、東京府またはその近隣にこれまでにない最大数のオリンピック観戦者のための宿泊施設を備えている。

　世界各国におかれては、次の点についてご安心願いたい。もし東京が1940年に選ばれたら、市だけではなく、国を挙げて直ちにその準備に取り掛かる。細大漏らさず準備を行う。その時を迎えるまでに、未完成あるいは不完全などという事態は決してない。このことを我々は約束することができる、なぜなら我々はわが国民のことをよくわかっているからである。卓越への間断なき強い願い―大国とならんとすることへの強い願いと同様に、国民は誇りと決然たる思いを持ってオリンピアードを迎えるための任務に取り組むであろう。

1940年、東京に！
東洋のスポーツ中心地が世界をいざなう！

TOKYO
SPORTS CENTER OF THE ORIENT

TOKYO MUNICIPAL OFFICE

1933

The pictures are offered by the courtesy of the Japan Amateur Athletic Association, the Jap. Gov. Railway's, the Kodokan, Tokyo Asahi and the Tokyo Nichi-nichi.

Printed by the Otsuka-Kogeisha, Tokyo

INVITATION

THE INTERNATIONAL OLYMPIC COMMITTEE

Honourable Gentlemen:

On behalf of the City of Tokyo and its people, I, the undersigned, Mayor of Tokyo, herewith beg to extend a most cordial invitation to the International Olympic Committee that the XIIth Olympic games be held in Japan during the year 1940, and that Tokyo be selected as the Olympic City. The city officials of Tokyo, and civic, business, and athletic organizations of Japan all join me in extending the above invitation.

We are anxiously and eagerly looking forward to the year 1940 when we may be granted the honour and pleasure to celebrate as host the XIIth Olympiad, making the same a notable event in the history of modern Games; and we shall also take that occasion to the 2,600th anniversary of the founding of the Empire of Japan, and thus contribute something unique to the Olympic movement.

We hereby give assurance that the City of Tokyo will take most seriously its responsibility of making the Olympic Games a great success; and that nothing will be left undone to make the XIIth Olympiad a great and glorious achievement in case Tokyo be selected as the Olympic City for 1940.

May the Olympic Torch light the way to the Orient; and may our more intimate contacts increase mutual understanding among the nations for the good of humanity, and may it lead to a purer and more enthusiastic and more courageous friendship.

I remain, Gentlemen,

Yours respectfully,

HIDEJIRO NAGATA
Mayor of Tokyo.

Tokyo, July 9th, 1932

are ample facilities for spectators, due to the fact that water carnivals are annual events in the capital. The water is generally smooth, for Tokyo Bay, which lies below, is almost completely landlocked, and in July and early August conditions should be ideal for the oarsmen of six continents.

For yachting there are two possible courses, one in lower Tokyo Bay, one to the west of the Miura Peninsula, where the larger boats will probably set their sails. Either is within an hour of the capital.

On the borders of Tokyo there are several country clubs and even more training grounds for army officers, so that the equestrian and marksmanship events could be cared for adequately even today, as could the indoor sports such as wrestling, fencing, boxing, weight-lifting and gymnastics. However, if the International Olympic Committee should designate Tokyo as host in 1940, all these installations will be categorically improved, an endeavor will be made to centralize them and the plant which will greet the world's athletes on their arrival here will be as perfect as the mind of man can compass. Already is excellent. Most of the work will be done to provide room for the record-breaking crowds which are expected.

Tokyo and the 12th Olympiad
In every counrty where Olympiads have been held the greatest worry of the host has been for the support of the public. Until Los Angeles, no Olympiad showed a profit. But Tokyo will have no anxiety on that score, for the public in this country is literally sports-mad. There is not a modern sport in this country which is not paying its own way. Even minor intercollegiate track and field, rugby, field hockey and association football meetings, which in the United States and other countries are notoriously poorly attended, in this country attract their thousands of devotees. If, Tokyo plays host to the Olympiad of 1940 every seat will be reserved at a premium for practically every event. No one who saw the milling thousands which bade godspeed to Japan's two shiploads of departing athletes in June of 1932, no one who witnessed the avidity with which the people absorbed news of the contests, no one who experienced the whole-hearted out-welling of national rejoicing upon the return of the contestants can doubt that the Empire of Japan as a whole, from the highest to the lowest, will support the games in Tokyo.

There is, of course, the question of weather. From almost every point of view, this can be considered ideal. For the winter sports there are the hard-packed snowfields of the Japan Alps, ideal for ski-ing and skating through many months of the winter. These are but four and five hours from Tokyo, on direct and comfortable railway lines. Accommodations for the spectators and contestants will be improved, but the ski runs are already up to high European standards.

The Ideal Weather for Olympic Games
From the point of view of weather, late July and early August are probably the evenest in Japan. There is a proverb that the annual rainy season ends when July arrives. This is not always true, but the first week of the month always sees its finish. From then until mid-August Tokyo generally enjoys unchanging sunny weather, practically perfect for athletic competition of all kinds. The high winds and uncertainties of the typhoon season do not commence until after the middle of August.

These, of course, are the main reasons which inspire Tokyo to believe that it can be a good host to the 1940 Olympiad. But there are others, to many minds much more important ones.

There is the fact that athletic interest is now world wide and that the Orient already has shown sufficient Olympic fidelity and athletic ability to be accorded recognition by the International Olympic committee. This is a point which we do not care to press unduly, for we believe it already to be recognized by all sports authorities.

Japan will be a unique and interesting setting for Olympic competition and to this fact the world cannot be blind. Opened but 60 years to Western civilization, much of the old remains. There are sharp and interesting con-

TOKYO
SPORTS CENTER OF THE ORIENT

EVER since the World War, that catastrophic punctuation mark in the story of mankind's progress, world-wide interest in sports has been developing. Human nature enjoys competition and the leaders of our modern nations, realizing that natural impulse, have been wise to encourage it, to direct it along sane, healthy, wholesome lines. The rseult has been a development of sports in the modern sense, which may be defined as a striving to develop the human body to the utmost speed, to the utmost rhythm, to the utmost display of power of which it is capable. It is not merely an exercise of brain and muscle for the enjoyment inherent in that exercise but a striving for perfection, for the ultimate.

This international development has not been restricted to one nation or to one continent. It now is world-wide. When the Olympic Games were revived in Athens in 1896 this was not the case. Of the 14 events scheduled, the United States won nine, Great Britain three. Up to then, Britain and America were the proverbial homes of sport. The interest of other nations was limited. This domination by two countries continued until the World War, but at Antwerp, Paris, Amsterdam and Los Angeles the broadening of the field of interest in sports was demonstrated progressively. In those four Olympiads every continent has been represented by champions. At Los Angeles seven different nations won team championships in various groups of events and 15 nations had teams which placed first, second or third. Twenty-nine of the 39 nations entered won places. Champions of 18 nationalities were crowned.

The showing of every nation at Los Angeles demonstrated that the world as a whole is taking sport seriously. Dilettantism has vanished. Training is being given profound study. With so much emphasis being placed on training, weather and other conditions and on the facilities for competition, a nation must be confident in its ability to conform to presume to be host to an Olympiad. But Tokyo, sports capital of the Orient, is confident and it invites the nations of the world to be its guests in 1940 for the Twelfth Olympiad of modern times. The purpose of this little booklet is to demonstrate the fitness of Japan's capital to receive the honor of being host.

Several questions must be studied. First of these, perhaps, is the matter of sports facilities. Second is the accommodation available for the public. Third is the matter of public interest. Fourth is the question of weather.

Tokyo's Facilities for Sports Even today Tokyo could dare be host to the athletes of the world, for the facilities for competition conform to the highest international standards. Japan's first city is a metropolis of 5,400,000, the third largest city in the world. Its sports center is the Outer Garden of the Meiji Shrine, a park destinies of his nation until 1912. In the outer gardens the Empire to Western civilization and who guided the destinies of his nation until 1912. In these outer gardens there is an athletic plant which compares favorably with any in the world. Two great stadia, one for track and field events, rugby, soccer and similar sports (capacity: 60,000) and the other for baseball (capacity: 55,000) are jammed with spectators throughout the year. Nearby is the Meiji Shrine Pool (capacity: 15,000) an installation made with the idea of giving the swimmers of this country conditions as like those they would meet in Los Angeles as possible.

Running through Tokyo is the River Sumida, where intercollegiate crew regatta are held. Along its course

ments to bankers and businessmen to locate in Yedo. Thus Yedo was promoted with a rush from the state of an inconsequential northern village to the temporal capital of the country. The actual capital remained, of course, in Kyoto, where the Emperor held his court, but the business and administration of the country was centered in the east. The regime of the Tokugawa Shoguns lasted for 268 years, until 1868, when the Meiji Restoration took place. The Emperor Meiji then removed the capital to Yedo, changing the name to Tokyo, which means "eastern capital," and took the Shogun's castle as the Imperial Palace.

To describe the rise of Tokyo to its present eminence would be to tell the story of modern Japan, a task which this small booklet cannot undertake. It must be noted, however, that the Meiji Restoration was coincident with the opening of Japan to the Western world and with the decision of its rulers to adopt what was found valuable in the alien civilization. The development started with a rush. In 1870 the first electric light plant was installed and operating. In 1872 the first railway line in the country, from Tokyo to the port of Yokohama 14 miles away, was opened. From those small beginnings the progress of Japan and of its capital was steady and rapid until 1923, when, at 11:58 o'clock on the morning of September 1, an earthquake started fires in more than 130 places and resulted in the destruction of more than half the city. Approximately 300,000 houses and other buildings were destroyed and the loss has been estimated at ¥3,700,000,000 (equal at par to £370,000,000, $1,850,000,000 or RM. 7,400,000,000).

Tokyo's Reconstruction

After every great fire it is the custom to say that the calamity was not unmixed with blessings. In the case of Tokyo this was literally true. At the time of the conflagration the city fathers were studying a comprehensive plan for the beautification of the city, for widening its streets, for improving the character of its buildings, public and otherwise. Then, the earthquake taught valuable lessons. It showed that modern structures of reinforced concrete were practically immune to the shocks. Thus, while the embers were still smouldering, orders were issued to make sure that the rebuilt Tokyo would be a more beautiful and a safer place. The citizens were told that, in certain districts, they could have permits to construct temporary buildings only. Later, new streets lines were established and permanent building permits were issued. In some sections only buildings of structural steel and reinforced concrete were permitted. The city spent more than ¥700,000,000, some of it directly, most of it in the form of subsidies and indemnities to property-owners whose land was taken to widen streets and improve the city. The result is that the Tokyo of 1933 is a city with wide streets and with many small areas enclosed in squares of concrete buildings, so that no fire in the future will be able to sweep the metropolis from end to end as did that of 1923.

In this connection an observation is important. The earthquake of 1923 came at the worst possible time, for housewives throughout the city were preparing the noonday meals and thousands of braziers were alight. The earthquake shocks tipped over the braziers and started a multitude of fires. Had the shocks come 30 minutes earlier or 30 minutes later the actual damage would have been relatively slight, for few houses in Tokyo were actually leveled by the earthquake. Thus the chances of a repetition of that disaster are small and have been made still more negligible by the wise city planning of the city fathers.

Rapid Expansion in Area and Population

In the years between the census of 1920 and that of 1930, the population of Tokyo increased but 100,000, partly due to the 1923 earthquake and fire but principally to the betterment in transportation facilities which made commuting from the suburbs not only possible but desirable. In those 10 years the suburbs gained 1,730,000 inhabitants and, taken together, grew more populous than the city itself. They included 84 towns and villages. As the years went by it became more and more evident that the interests of

trasts. For this reason, if for no other, the world is interested in Japan. To set the Twelfth Olympiad against this background of a civilization thousands of years old, against the national celebration of the Empire's 2600th anniversary under a single Imperial Dynasty, would be the lend to the competitions an added interest, a complementary attraction.

Japan no more is on the edge of the world. Improved communications have brought it within two weeks of any competing country save Australia—and Australia is farther from Europe or the United States than from Japan. The Pacific Ocean is the center of th eworld—and Japan is the focal point upon the Pacific—with Tokyo the center of Japan, geographically, culturally, economically and from the point of view of sports.

GREATER TOKYO

SO much emphasis has been placed upon the differences between Japanese and Western customs that it is only with difficulty that the foreign visitor to these shores recovers from the shock of Tokyo's modernity. He finds a modern city on a range of low hills, beautiful public buildings, great commercial establishmenst, well-kept streets, an efficient and rapid electric line and trolley service, taxicabs in abundance, a water system equal to any in the world, comfortable European-style hotels, parks, schools, factories, theatres—everything which he has learned to look upon as a concomitant of a strictly Western culture.

If his reading about this country has been confined to the observations that the Japanese carpenter builds the roof of a house first and pulls plane and saw to him instead of pushing them away in the Western manner, that the books of this country are printed from top to bottom of the page instead of from left to right; if his mind is a pot-pourri of geisha, temples, shrines, sylvan waterfalls, peaceful gardens into which the sights nad wounds of the workaday world world never intrude, Confucianism, Bushido, the Forty-Seven Ronin and honorofic particles placed before every word—as many romantic writers mistakenly insist—then the shock to his preconceived notions upon reaching Tokyo must be tremendous.

Make no mistake about it: Japan has an ancient civilization and is proud of it. It is a cultural legacy which the Empire will do everything to retain. But culture is hardly a tangible thing. It is not what obtrudes to the view of the visitor. And Japan today is a modern nation. It has taken those attributes of Western progress which seemed best fitted to its needs, has adapted them, has improved on some. Tokyo today is one of the most beautiful cities in the world. Much of Old Japan remains, to be sure, but it is held in the hearts and in the minds of the people rather than in the outer forms. There are temples and shrines which breathe the air of the olden days, which are instinct with the devotion and reverential scholarship of thousands of years of religious seclusion. There are gardens tucked away here and there. But, although the soul of Japan may have a secure basis in the past, the body of Japan marches in the present and the mind of Japan looks into the future. And Tokyo is the leader.

Tokyo's Origin A little more than 1,000 years ago, Tokyo was a wilderness in a remote corner of eastern Japan, far removed from the flourishing cultures of Kyoto and Nara. Later a small village sprang up and about 466 years ago Ota Dokan, a feudal lord, picked upon it as a site for his castle, because of its strategic situation. In 1590 Tokugawa Iyeyasu was namde feudal overlord of the eight provinces about Yedo, as Tokyo was then called. Ten years later he became Shogun (warlord) of all Japan and chose Yedo for his capital. He forced the feudal lords of the country to leave their families in the city and to spend part of their time with him. At the same time he offered induce-

these communities would be served by amalgamation with Tokyo and on October 1, 1932, the thirty-fourth anniversary of self-governmnet in the capital, 82 of them were absorbed. Twenty new wards were created, making a total of 35, and the area of the city rose from 85 square kilometers to 553. Taking Tokyo Central Station as the center, the radius of the ctiy is 10 miles. On October 1, 1930, the date of the last national census, the territory now included in Tokyo had a population of 4,970,839. By October 1, 1932, this had risen to 5,298,957 and now, in May, 1933, is certainly over 5,400,000, making it the third largest city in the world, topped only by Greater London and New York and exceeding Berlin and Chicago.

Modern Improvements
Building in and improvements to Tokyo have not been completed. Unsatisfied with the present excellent condition of the city, which shows no signs of the trials through which it has passed, the authorities have planned to spend ¥860,000,000 more over the next 15 years. Of this total, ¥330,000,000 will go to build roads and bridges. Tokyo now is working on a comprehensive road building plan which will make it one of the most adequately equipped cities in the world when it is complete. Before the earthquake the total area of streets in the city was 925,621 square miles. When the new plans are complete, the area will be increased by 3,600,000 square miles, almost fourfold. A basic trunk boulevard of 33 to 44 meters in width is to run from north to south. This is almost completed now and much of it is in use. In addition, there will be a transverse trunk street almost as wide. Both these main arteries will be flanked with slightly narrower streets to relieve congestion. A great boulevard girdling the city will be complete in the next four or five years, connected by radial boulevards to the Tokyo Station, the heart of the city planning scheme. In addition to these, 52 streets with a total length of 119 kilometers and widths of 22 meters or more will be constructed throughout the city, supplemented by 122 smaller streets or widths less than 22 meters. When the street plan is complete, streets will occupy 27 per cent of the area served, comparing favorably with London, Paris and Berlin. Much of this work will have been completed by the time Tokyo plays host to the 1940 Olympiad.

Tokyo is a city of many bridges, with the nine great spans across the Sumida River attracting the bulk of the attention. Canals cut the city into checkerboards and during the reconstruction of the city 523 street bridges had to be constructed. Most of these were designed with an eye to civic beautification as well as to utility.

Temples, Shrines and Parks
In the days before Tokyo became a modern city living conditions were not so congested. Temples and shrines all had parks attached and most private dwellings had gardens. But real estate costs have mounted so rapidly that this no longer is possible and the city authorities have been forced to provide for parks in their plans. There are now 100 parks in Tokyo, including several exceedingly large ones. Foremost of these is the Outer Garden of the Meiji Shrine, previously mentioned, with two stadia, a swimming pool, an outdoor arena for basketball, boxing, fencing and wrestling and many other facilities. This is adjacent to the vast Yoyogi Parade Ground and to the Shrine gardens proper. Shiba Park, formerly the grounds of one of the great Buddhist temples but now owned principally by the city; Uyeno Park, with its museums and zoological gardens; Asakusa Park, Hibiya Park, with its open air bandstands and amphitheaters, and the great parks along both sides of the lower Sumida River are perhaps the most important of the other public gardens in the city, for they are all great open places in rather congested parts of Tokyo.

Modern Buildings
It is difficult to give a reader a fully-formed idea of Tokyo and its modern facilities, for the activities of the city and the improvements it has effected cover so many phases of the citizen's life. There are, for example, 117 three-storied earthquaqe-proof buildings which house primary schools, all handsome structures. Tokyo Imperial

University, Keio University, Waseda University, the Tokyo University of Literature and Science and many other institutions of high learning are situated in the capital, all with excellent plants both for academic work and athletics. The Government buildings, especially those which have been constructed since the 1923 disaster, are imposing tributes to the skill of their architects. The art museum in the Outer Gardens of the Meiji Shrine and the new Imperial Diet building are probably as impressive to the foreign eye as any buildings in modern style of which Japan can boast. The city's great banks, including the Government institutions, are triumphs of Western-style architecture adapted to Japanese uses. Chief of these are the Bank of Japan, Mitsui Bank, Yokohama Specie Bank, Mitsubishi Bank, First Bank and Hypothec Bank of Japan. Impressions of these and of other great buildings in Tokyo, among which may be mentioned the new Central Postoffice, the Postal Life Insurance Building, the Marunouchi Building, the Tokyo Marine and Fire Insurance Company building and the Tokyo Stock Exchange, can be conveyed only by the eye. An endless amount of description would be fruitless, no matter how well done. Accordingly, for the physical aspects of the capital, the reader must turn to the photographs which accompany this text.

Public Health

Tokyo is rich in excellently-equipped hospitals. The largest of these are the Fraternity Hospital, built with American contributions for relief following the 1923 fire and earthquake; the Red Cross Hospital, heavily endowed by the Imperial Household, and St. Luke's International Medical Center, which has just moved into a new building. In addition to these there are literally dozens of smaller hospitals, most of them private and well endowed, and several free municipal hospitals, with a total of 1,000 beds and facilities for handling 1,000 out-patients a day.

Health supervision in Tokyo is thorough and compares well with systems in the capitals of Europe. In a recent year, for example, only 21,710 cases of epidemic diseases were reported, due to prompt action on the part of the authorities. When it is considered that more than half of these were of dysentery and that there is literally no control over this in the neighbouring China, the record of the health authorities is remarkable.

Work on the construction of sewers was seriously delayed by the 1923 earthquake but now is being taken up with new vigor and during the next 15 years ¥190,000,000 will be spent on them. Garbage disposal plants have recently been improved and the past 10 years have seen great improvements in removal with the establishment of 27 depots in various parts of the city.

Educational Facilities

Tokyo today has 1,602 educational institutions, of which 842 are public and 760 private, including 117 universities, colleges and higher technical schols. Tokyo City alone operates 793 kindergartens, primary schools, middle schools, girls' higher schools and industrial schools, not to mention night schools for the children of the poor, who work in the daytime.

Social Works

While laws and customs of Japan with regard to dismissal allowances have operated to keep employment fairly stable, so that this country has no such problems as have been bothering the United States and Europe, persons in need of public aid will probably always be with us. Thus, Tokyo has a slum population of 317,090. Congested living conditions naturally are always a menace to public health and the city government is doing its utmost to correct them. There are now 98 district welfare offices, the homes of 1,800 welfare committees, which are assisting the poor to find work and are trying to better their physical surroundings. Tokyo has 921 social work groups, with 304 under the city's management.

Modern Water Supply System

How many visitors to Japan have been told by ignorant fellow-passengers that it was unwise to drink the water in Japan without boiling it? Nothing can be farther from the truth. Since 1911 Tokyo has had a water-supply system second to none in the world.

In that year work on the 20-year product of the Tama reservoir was completed. The upper reaches of the river were led to the Yodobashi filter beds and Tokyo was assured a supply of good water. But the supply was adequate only for the population of that time. The authorities recognized this and five years later began work on the Murayam reservoir, 40 miles from the center of the city. This project, completed in 1926, gave old Tokyo (before the 1932 amalagamation) an adequate supply, but work is now in progress on two other supplies, so that all the towns and villages now within the city limits will have the advantage of a pure and adequate flow throughout the year.

Traffic Facilities Enough has been said of the up-to-date aspect of Tokyo's streets, parks and buildings. What, now, of traffic facilities? These are complete and comprehensive. The electric lines of the Imperial Government Railway circle the city and give rapid and convenient connection with all the neighbouring cities. The round-the-city lines, in concentric circles, are 96 kilometers in length. Within the limits of Tokyo there are also 200 kilometers of private electric lines, owned by private companies, plus municipal trolley cars and bus lines. All these carry more than 1,000,000,000 passengers a year. There is also the new subway, now reaching from Asakusa Park, the great amusement center, to the middle of the city. The company which has undertaken this work hsa been reporting profits steadily ever since the first two-mile stretch was opened and therefore there seems to be no reason for believing that it will not be able to carry out all its plans by the time the Twelfth Olympiad comes to Tokyo. This plans call for a loop about the heart of the city and branch lines which will bring every part of the metropolis within a few minutes of its center. This will be a great aid to communication in 1940, for the Olympic Stadium-to-be, now about 20 minutes by taxicab from the hotel and business center and 30 minutes by Government line, will be but six or seven minutes distant by subway.

In dealing with communications, it is necessary to include the air srevice. There are three terminals in Tokyo or near it, with the Haneda Airport quite convenient to all the hotels.

Hotel Accommodation While the most optimistic booster for Tokyo must admit that present, hotel space could not possibly stretch to meet the demands which would be put upon it by the Olympic crowds were Tokyo to be made the 1940, host, the city and its environs can possibly do as well in this respect as any in the world. In Tokyo proper there are but six foreign-style hotels, but the city is fortunate in having at its doors a district of Japan which is more favored than any other for resorts. This is Kanagawa Prefecture, in which are located Hayama, Zushi, Kamakura, Miyanoshita, Oiso, Odawara, Hakone and dozens of other towns which make a specialty of catering to foreign guests. It also includes Yokohama. Thus the visitor to the games will be able to find rooms in picturesque hotels throughout the surrounding district, generally with sea bathing close at hand, and yet be within an hour of the capital and its international contests.

Special accommodations, of course, would be arranged for the athletes and quite probably these facilities would be extended to coaches, trainers and other officials of the various delegations as well. The Western world may rest assured that, in the event that Tokyo is chosen, every effort will be made, long in advance, to provide accommodations for any crowd likely to come from abroad to witness the Olympiad. Already the framework is in existence.

English, the Second Language in Japan One point is likely to cause hesitation. In the past, Olympiads have been held in countries in which the second language, at least, was one known to a majority of the competitors and most of the visitors. One can imagine the Olympic officials shaking their heads and wondering how the athletes and visitors will fare in a country such as Japan. This should not be a cause for concern. English is the

second language in Japan and, while one cannot contend that everyone speaks it readily, the fact remains that all college and university students, those with whom the visiting athletes are most likely to come into contact, handle it well enough for simple conversations. In the hotels and inns at least one clerk will always be found who manages the language with facility.

Recreation Facilities

Tokyo is not without recreational facilities for the visitor. There are, of course, the usual tourist attractions, temples, shrines, monuments and museums. But these are day-time diversions. There is also much to occupy the evenings. Tokyo has about 12 first-run motion picture houses playing foreign film exclusively, in addition to perhaps 60 smaller theatres which show Japanese film. In addition to these, there are the theaters specializing in the Kabuki drama, including music-posture plays of an earlier age and the so-called modern Kabuki. Usually two or three houses are playing revues in the Western manner, quite comprehensible to an outlander, while scattered through the city are perhaps a dozen small revue theaters which eschew the spectacular and concentrate on humor, largely in pantomime. Foreign visitors without a word of Japanese have often found these quite comprehensible and much more entertaining than the elaborate revues on the Parisian pattern played in the larger theaters.

Tokyo also boasts 10 or 12 dance halls in which Western music is *de rigueur*, all under close police supervision, while perhaps 100 of the thousands of bars and cafes in the city will be found attractive by foreigners. The city does not boast of these and keeps them under careful conrtol, but honesty compels the admission that, in the absence of cabaret forms of entertainment, our visitors find them vastly pleasing and entertaining.

Will You Be There?

Such is the story of modern Tokyo, its origins, its troubles, its present condition. It is a city which has made immense progress, while still is advancing at an almost unbelievable rate. Perhaps— and this is by no means unlikely—this poor description of the capital of Japan will have become nearly unrecognizable in the seven short years before the trumpets sound for the Twelfth Olympiad. The Tokyo of 1940 may be as little like the Tokyo of today as that of 1926.

In this little book an effort has been made to show that Tokyo is a city fully qualified to be host to an Olympiad. It has a fully equipped athletic plant, surpassed by few in the world. It has an athletic record which gives it a right to the honor. It has a populace which will extend itself to honor its foreign guests and which will flock to the amphitheaters, guaranteeing in advance the success of the undertaking. Tokyo is a modern city, a clean city, a metropolis in Western fashion against the panorama of an age-old civilization. It provides fascinating contrasts, a daily object lesson in what can be accomplished by intelligent planning and courageous execution. It is a ciyt which has within its borders the facilities for one of the most memorable Olympic Games of modern times and within its borders or a stone's throw away the accommodations for the greatest Olympic attendance the world has seen.

Of one thing the world may rest assured: If Tokyo is chosen for 1940 not only the city but the nation as a whole will start work immediately. Nothing will be neglected. Nothing will be left half-done or incomplete when the time comes. This we can promise, for we know our people. Their continual urge is to excel—and they will tackle the job of entertaining an Olympiad as proudly and as resolutely as they have that of becoming a World Power.

Tokyo in 1940!

The sports capital of the Orient invites you!

Niju-bashi, the Main Gateway to the Imperial Palace

Ote Gate of the Imperial Palace

The Inner Moat at Uchisakurada Gate of the Imperial Palace

Tokyo Station, the Entrance of the City

Air View of Sukiyabashi District

Air view of Marunouchi, a Business Center of Tokyo

The New Parliamentary Building

The Street along side of the Tokyo City Hall

Marunouchi Street

The Boulevard in the Outer Gardens of Meiji Shrine

The Boulevard to the Imperial Palace

Sukiyabashi District Viewed from the Canal

Nihonbashi District Viewed from the Canal

Benkei-bashi Bridge, a Typical Peculiar Japanese Bridge over the Moat near Akasaka-mitsuke

Kiyosu-bashi Bridge over the Sumida River

Eitai-bashi Bridge over the Sumida River

Tokyo Imperial Museum

Tokyo Art Gallery

Emperor Meiji Memorial Picture Gallery

Tokyo Imperial University

Waseda University

Keio University

Hibiya Park

Inokashira Natural Park

Former Shiba Detached Palace Garden

Sumida Riverside Park

Air View of the Maruyama Water Reservoir
(The maximum effective capacity, 12,354,955 cubic metres)

Ochanomizu Railway Station and Vicinity

Haneda International Air Port

Meiji Shrine, Dedicated to the Great Emperor Meiji

Earthquake Memorial Hall, Built by the City for the Gommemoration of the Ashes of the Victims in the Seismic Disaster of 1923

Yasukuni Shrine, a Pantheon for the Illustrious Dead who Have Fallen on Various Battlefields Since the Restoration of the Country, and its Biggest Torii in Japan

Ginza Street, the Fifth
Avenue of Tokyo

Night View of Shinjuku
Street

Theatre Street in Asakusa Park, Coney Island of Tokyo

Kabukiza Theatre, in Which the Unique Kabuki Drama is Staged

Interior of the Theatre

The Imperial Hotel

Interior of a Department Store in Tokyo

The Japanese Olympic Team, carrying the flag of the Rising Sun granted by H.I.H. Prince Chichibu,
being borne along the track at the opening ceremony of the Xth Olympic Games.
Los Angeles, July, 30, 1932

Air View of the Sport Arenas in the Outer Gardens of Meiji Shrine

Meiji Shrine Stadium with a Seating Capacity of 60,000

800 Metre Race at Meiji Shrine Stadium

Girl's High Jump   Hop-Step-Jump

Finish Line of 400 Metre Race

High Hurdle Race

Swimming Pool at the Outer Garden of Meiji Shrine (Capacity 15,000)

Swimming Race at the Meiji Shrine Swimming Pool

Night Swimming Race at the Meiji Shrine Swimming Pool

Water Polo Match at the Meiji Shrine Swimming Pool

Girl's High Diving

Tamagawa Swimming Pool

Tsukishima Municipal Swimming Pool   Shiba Municipal Swimming Pool

Eights Race

Air View of the Sumida, an Ideal Regatta Course

Fours Race

Okurayama Schunze near Sapporo, Hokkaido

Sankakuyama Slope, Sapporo, Hokkaido

North Japan Alps Viewed from Mt. Nekodake, near Tokyo

Skate Race at Kiyotaki-gawara Skate Links, Nikko

Takamatsu-ike Skate Links, near Morioka   Girl's Artistic Skating

Mass Game at the Meiji Shrine Stadium

Gymnastics at the Meiji Shrine Stadium

Boxing at the Hibiya Municipal Amphitheater

Tennis Match at Sannencho Tennis Court

Rugby Game at the Meiji Shrine Stadium

Hockey at the Meiji Shrine Stadium

Indoor Basket-ball at the Tokyo Y.M.C.A. Hall

Court for Basket-ball and Ballet-ball at the Outer Garden
of Meiji Shrine

Girl Students Practising Archery in a School Yard

Ballet-Ball Match of Girls at the Meiji Shrine Court

Air View of the Baseball Ground (Capacity, 65,000) at the Outer Garden of Meiji Shrine

Air View of Kasumigaseki Golf Links, near Tokyo

Classical Sports of Japan

Besides the various forms of sports introduced from abroad we have in Japan other time-honoured ones such as "Judo", "Kendo", "Sumo", etc. These are arts in which the display of skill and physical strength has been refined by the practice and experience of ages.

'Judo' or 'Jujutsu' an original and unique sport of Japan

Archery in formal style

'Sumo' the Japanese wrestling

'Kendo', the Japanese fencing

'Yabusame', an exhibition shooting on horse-back.
The archery is dressed in the costume
of feudal days

Old style of swimming handicapped
by the heavy burden—a gigantic
flag fastened to a long
bamboo pole

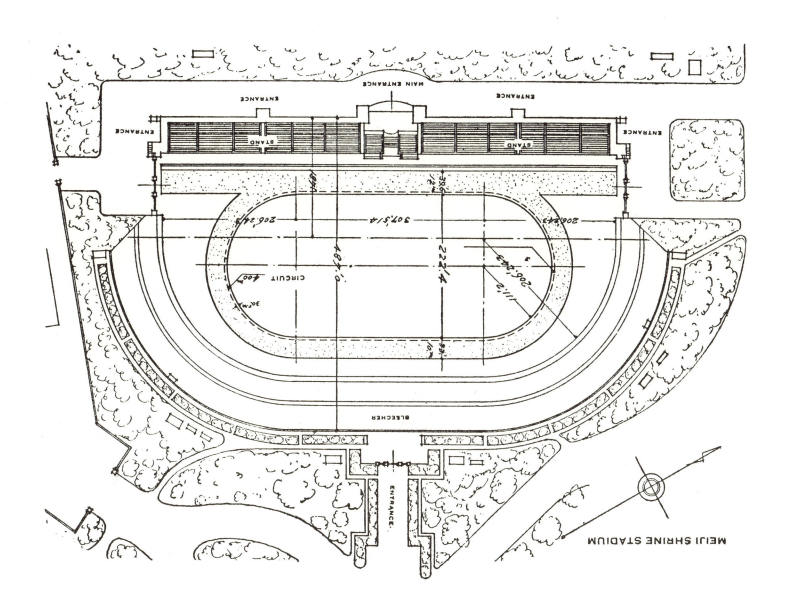

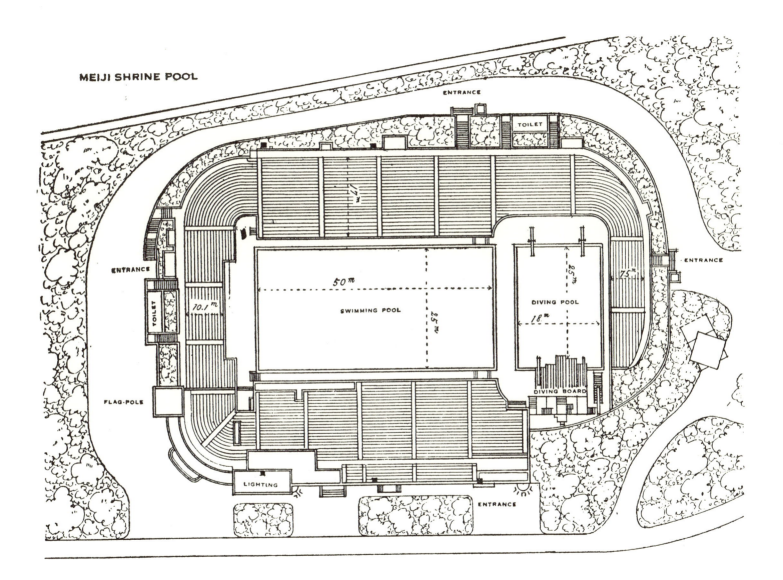